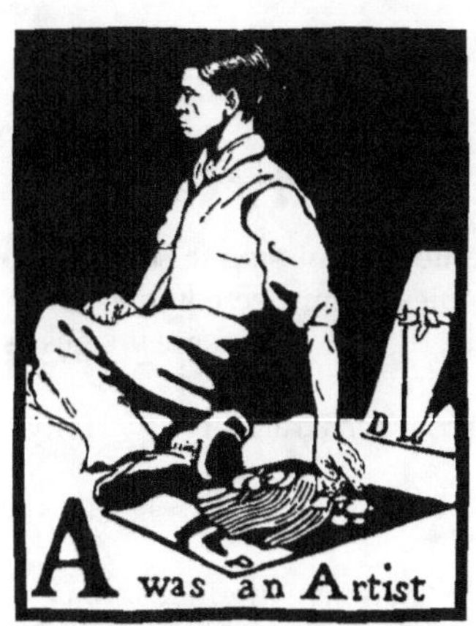

An Alphabet

By William Nicholson

Original lithographs translated by Holly Ollivander.

ISBN: 978-1-905605-43-9

www.velluminous.com

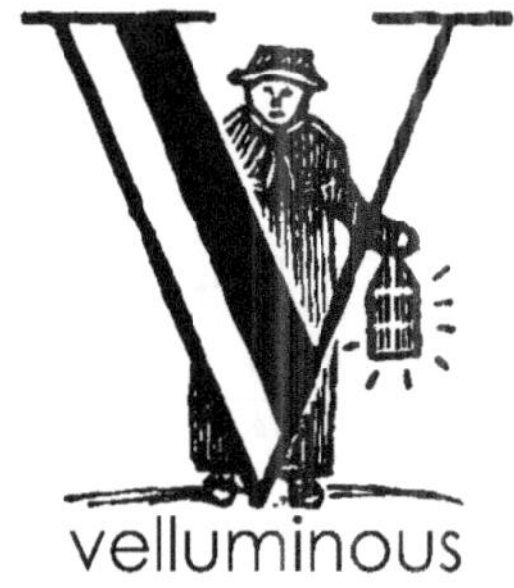

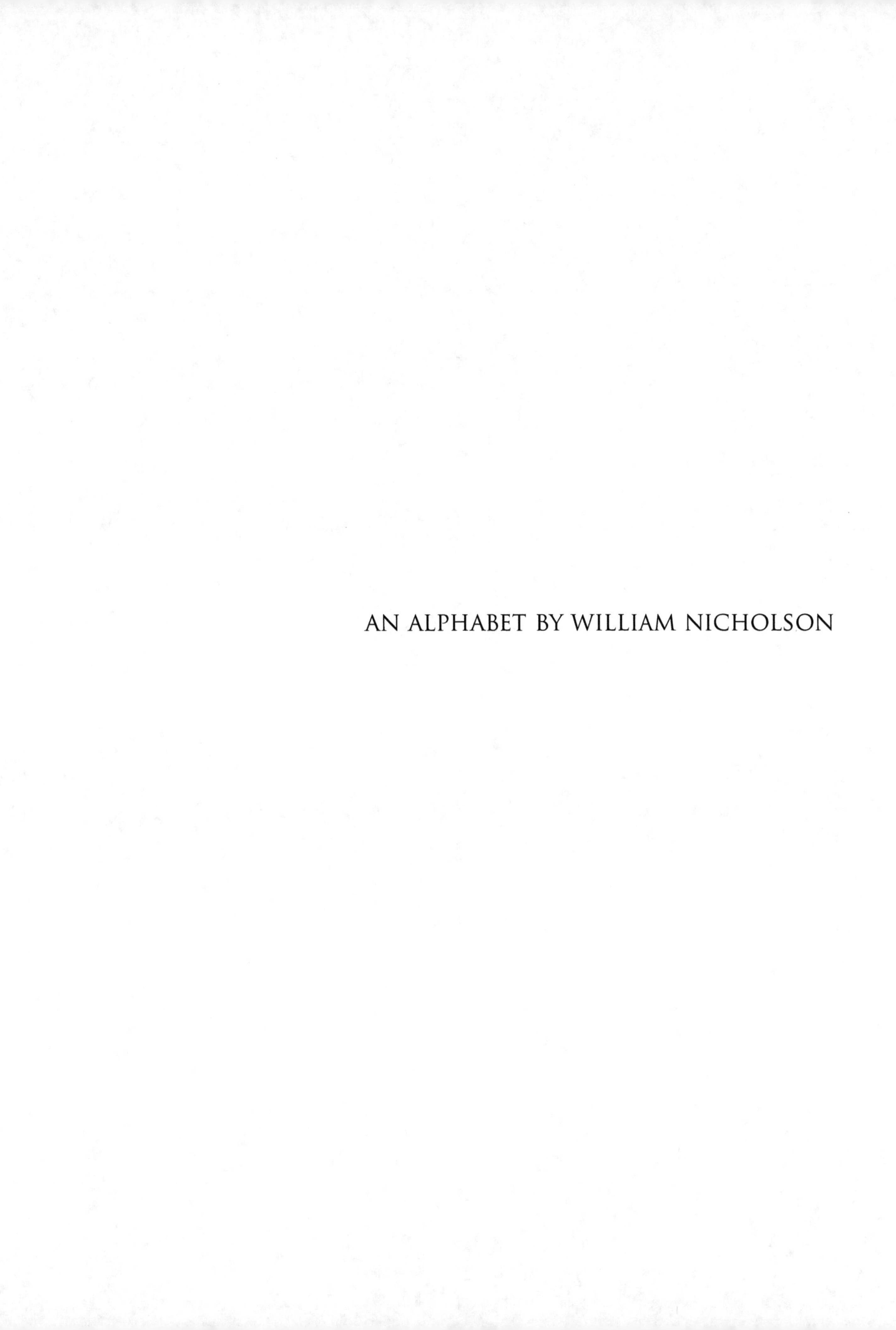

AN ALPHABET BY WILLIAM NICHOLSON

William Nicholson (5th February 1872 – 16th May 1949) was a painter, engraver, graphic artist, stained glass craftsman, author, illustrator and theatre set designer with an astonishing gift: he pursued light and pinned down shadow with a visual brevity and mastery rarely seen in Western Art. The images within this book still stand as an exemplar of how to distil the essence of three dimensions into two colours, proving a continual inspiration to generations of graphic artists since.

It is our pleasure to present, in a scanner-friendly printed format, these images as Nicholson originally saw them, and before time and pigment altered them forever.

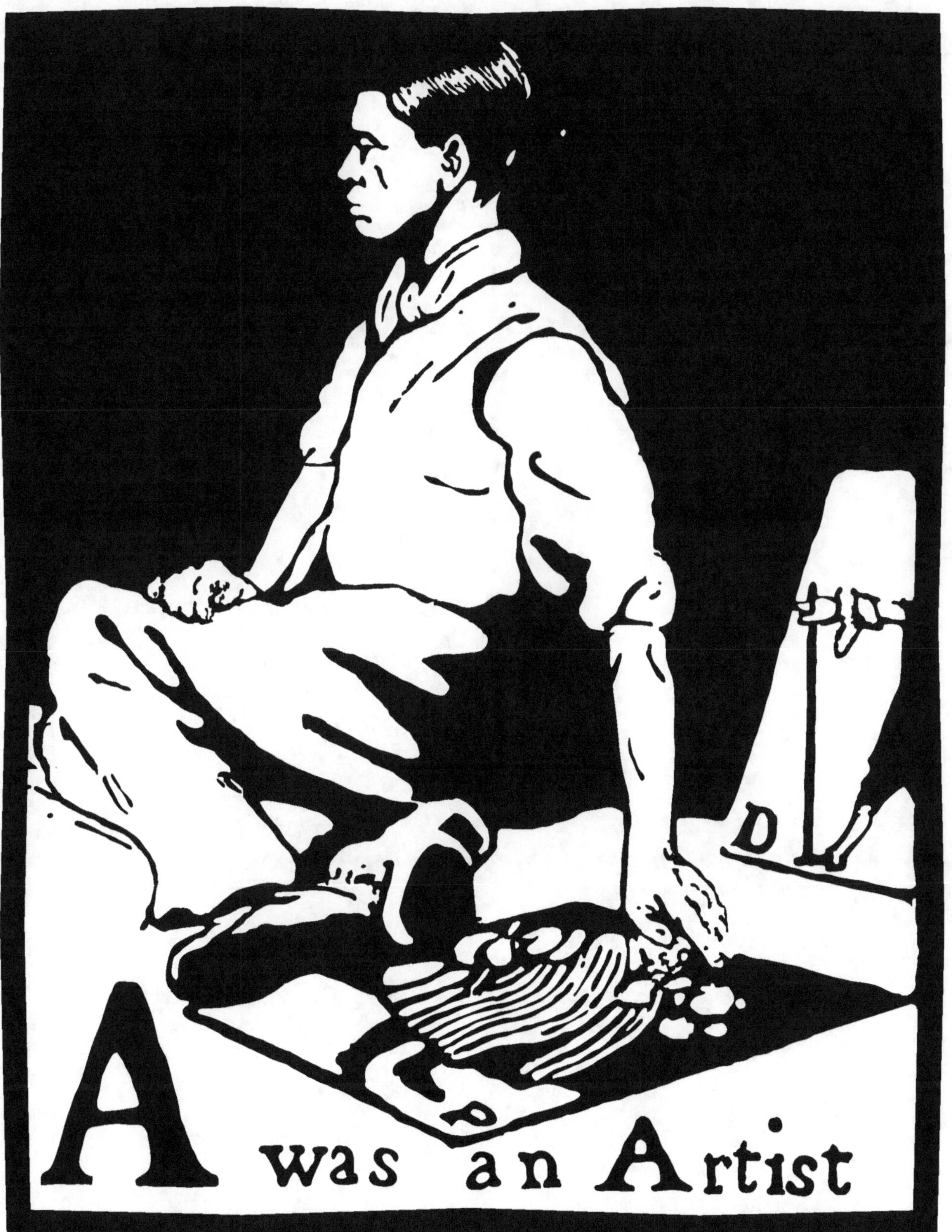

A was an Artist

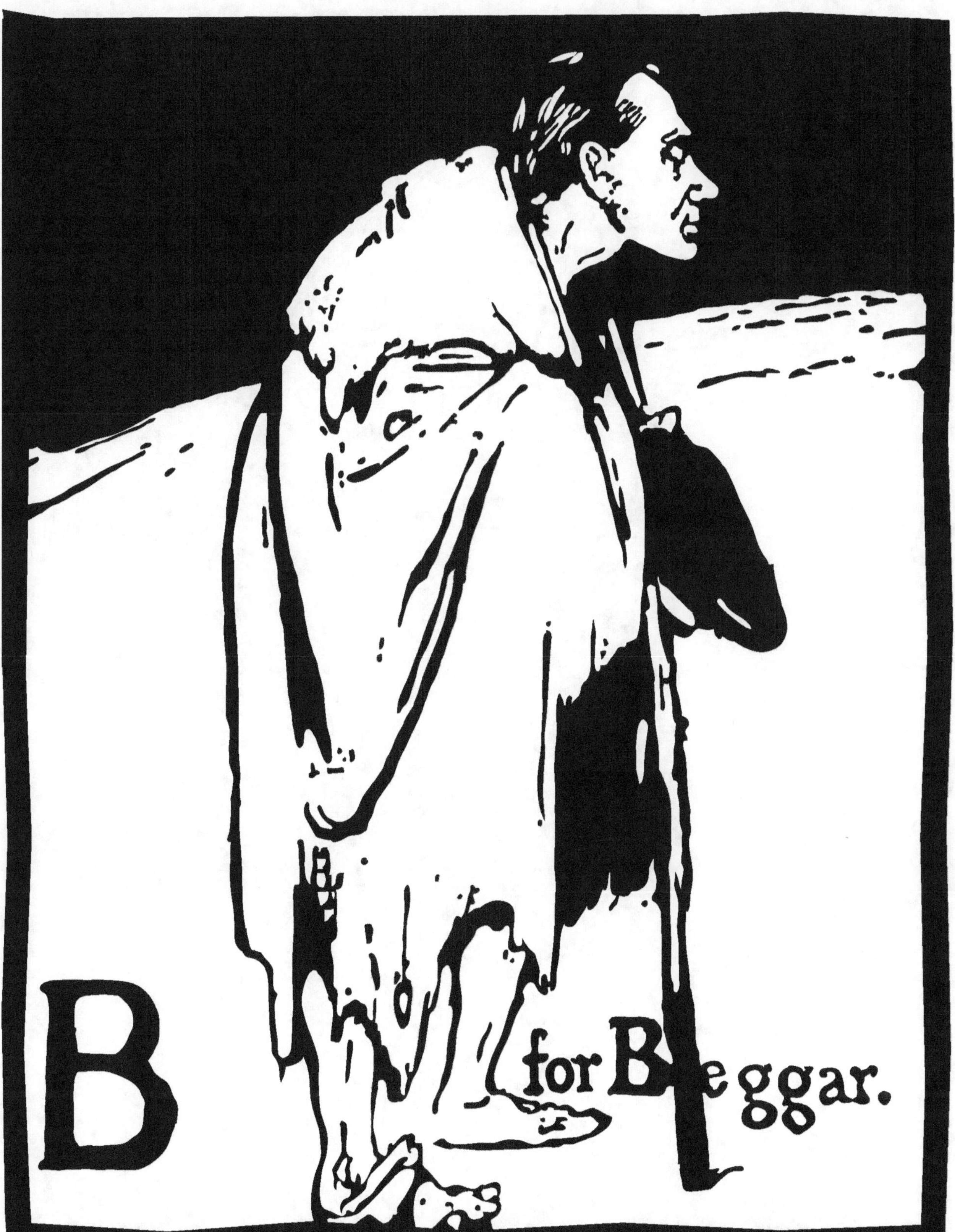

B
for Beggar.

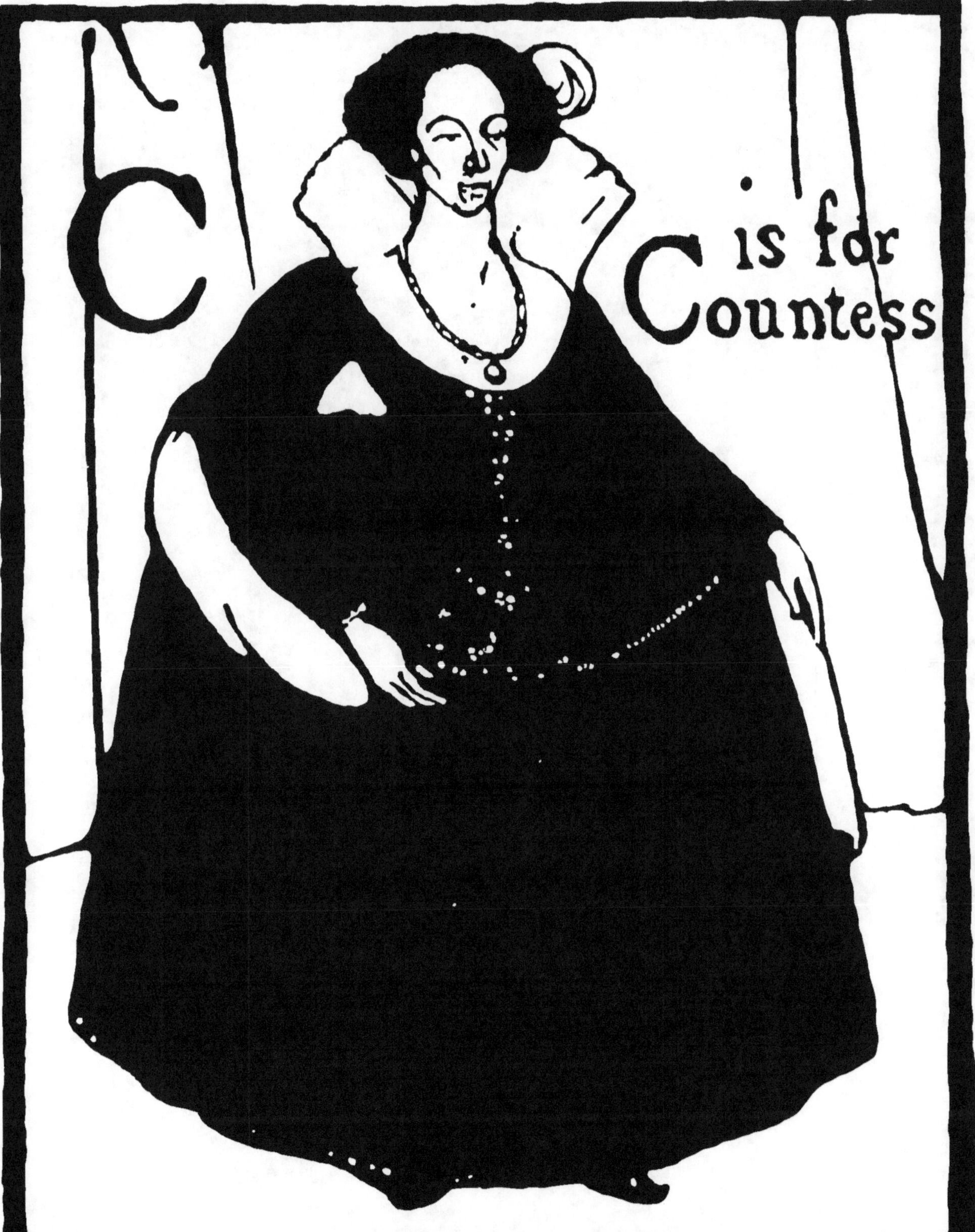

C
C is for
Countess

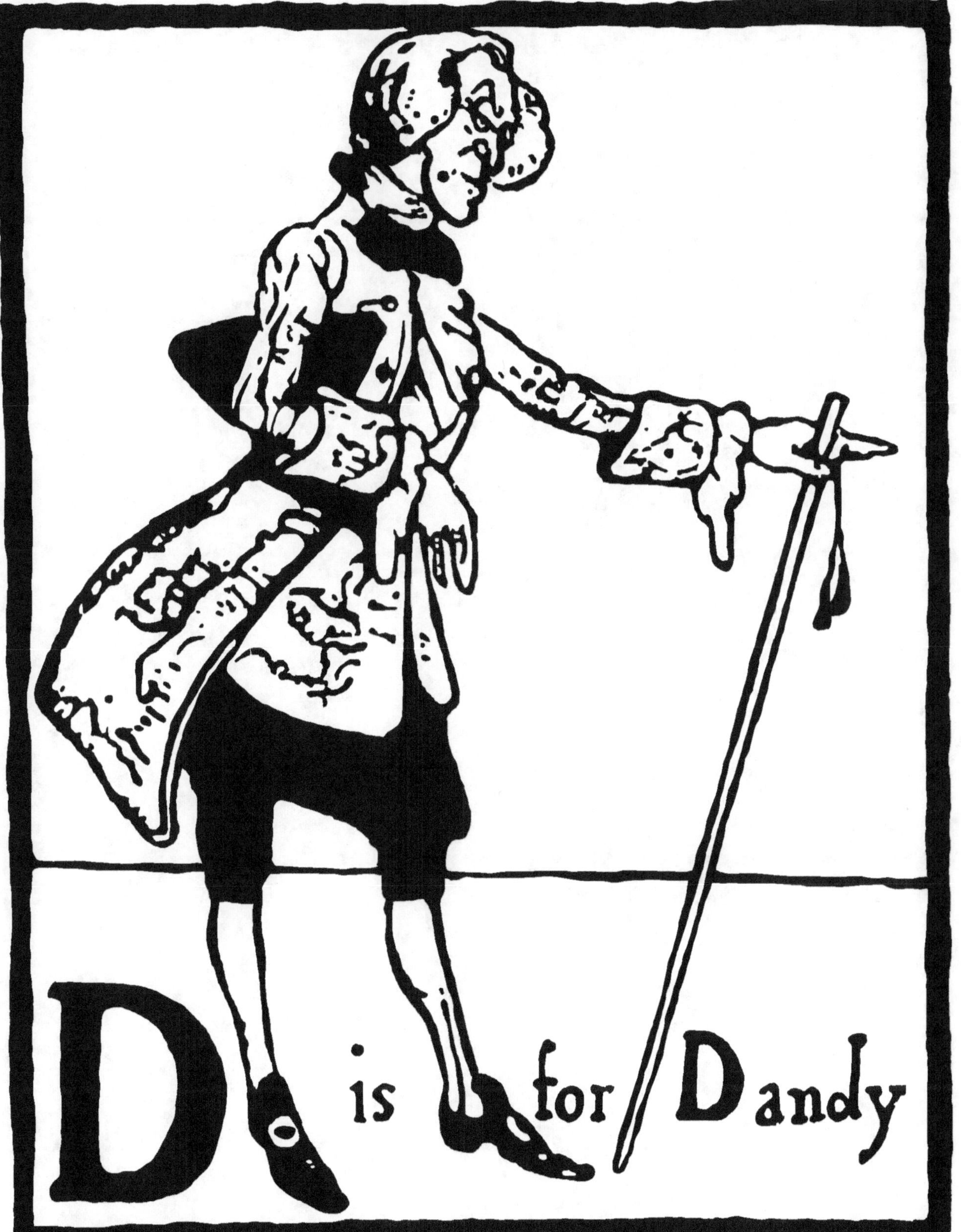

D is for Dandy

E for Executioner

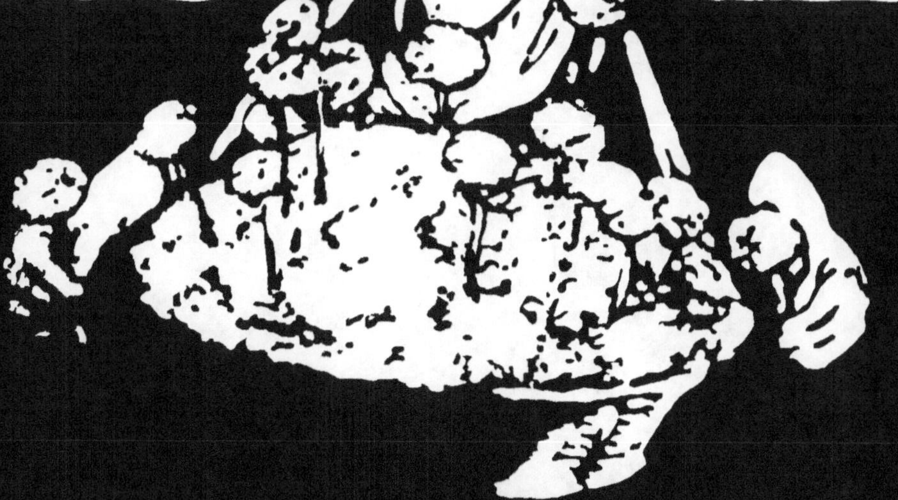

F is for Flower Girl.

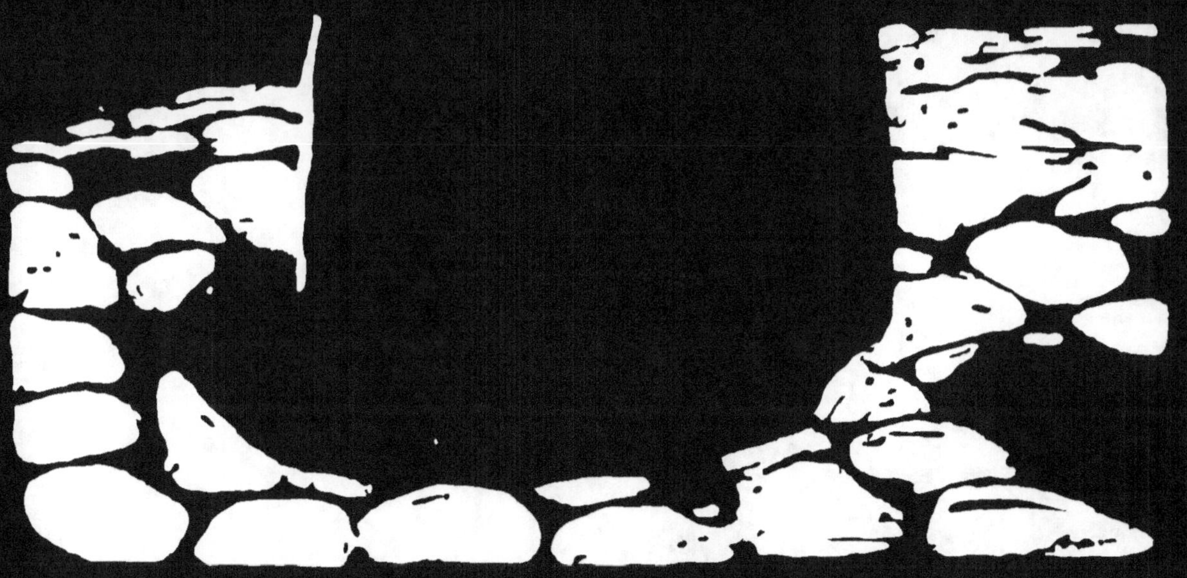

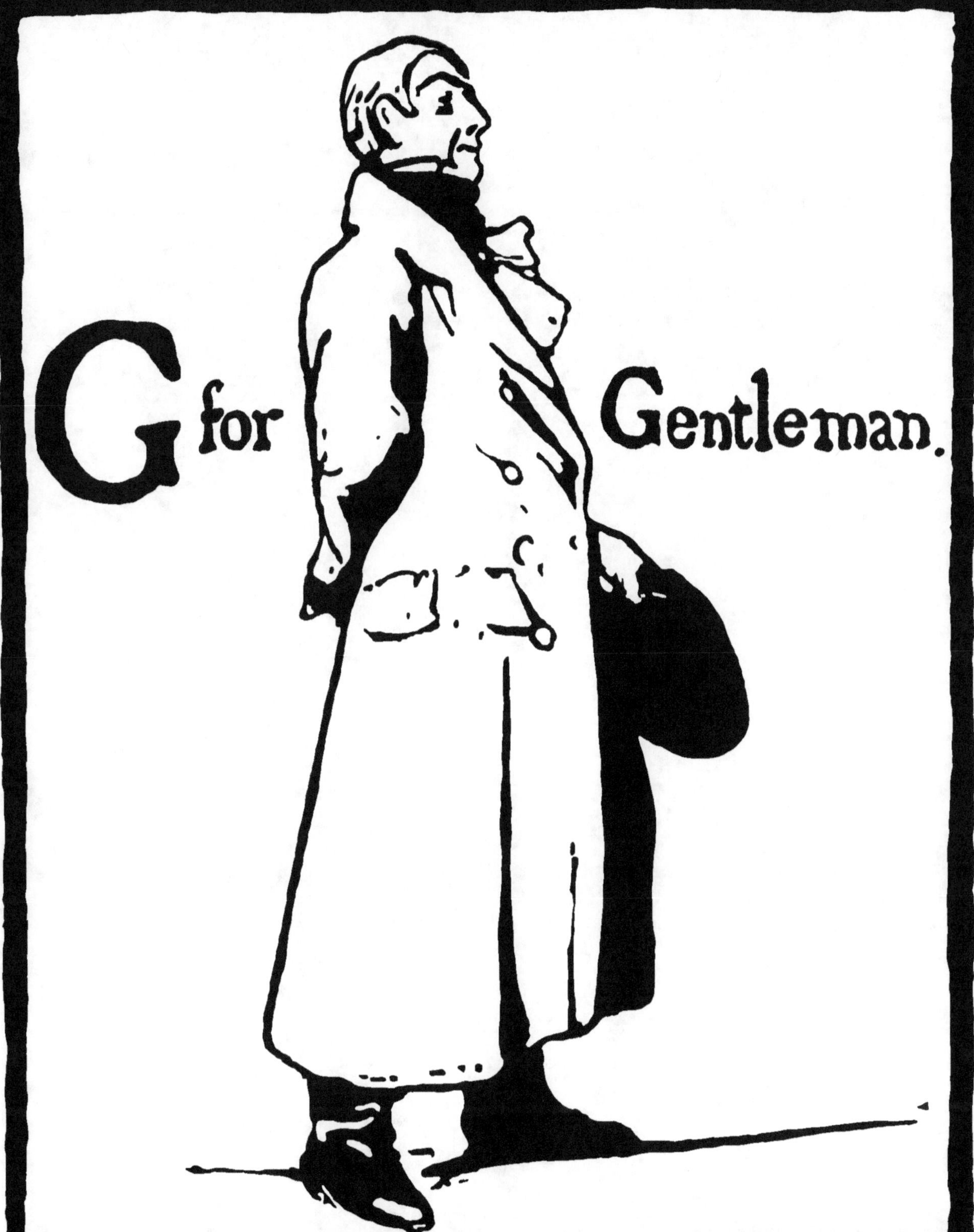

G for Gentleman.

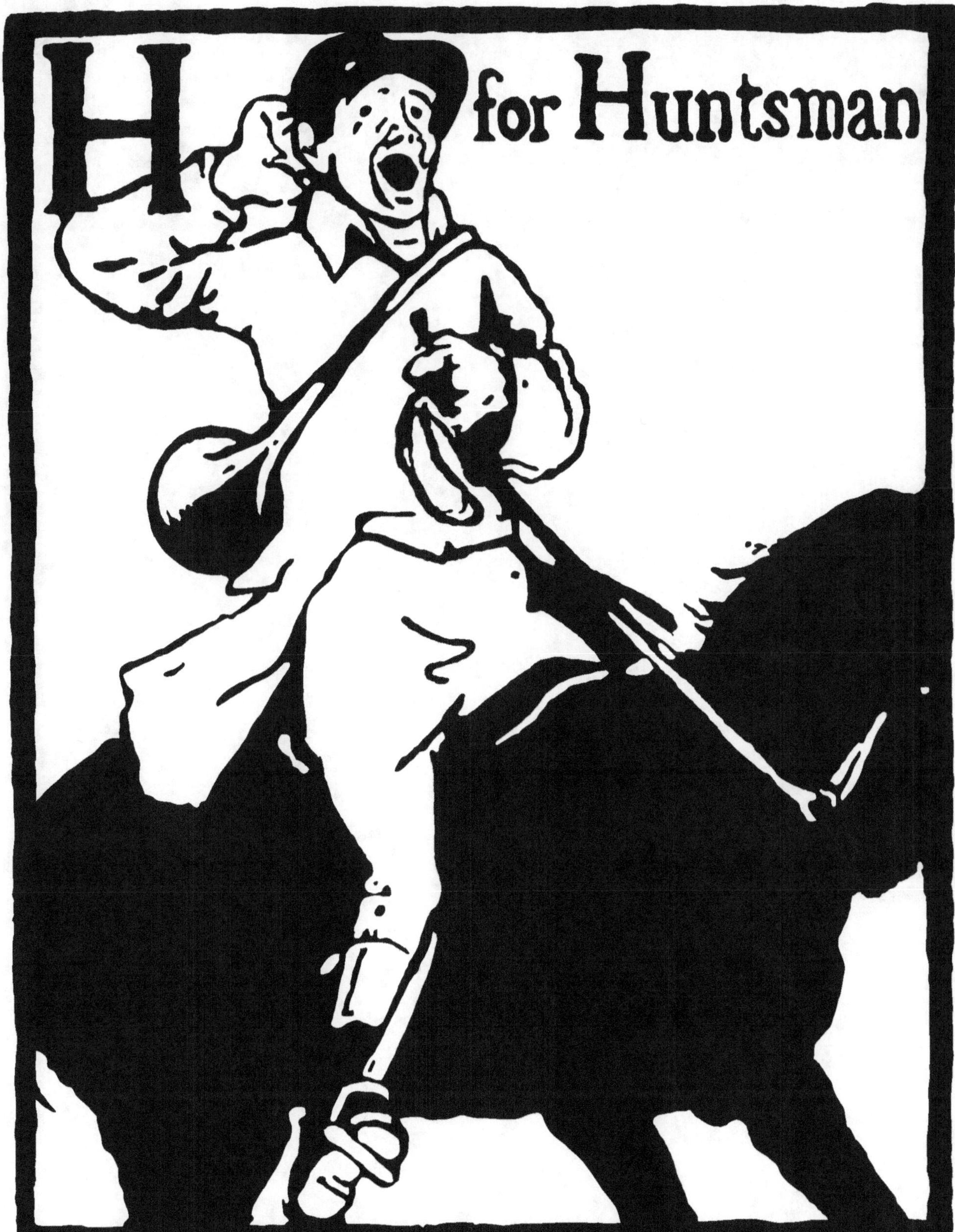
H
for Huntsman

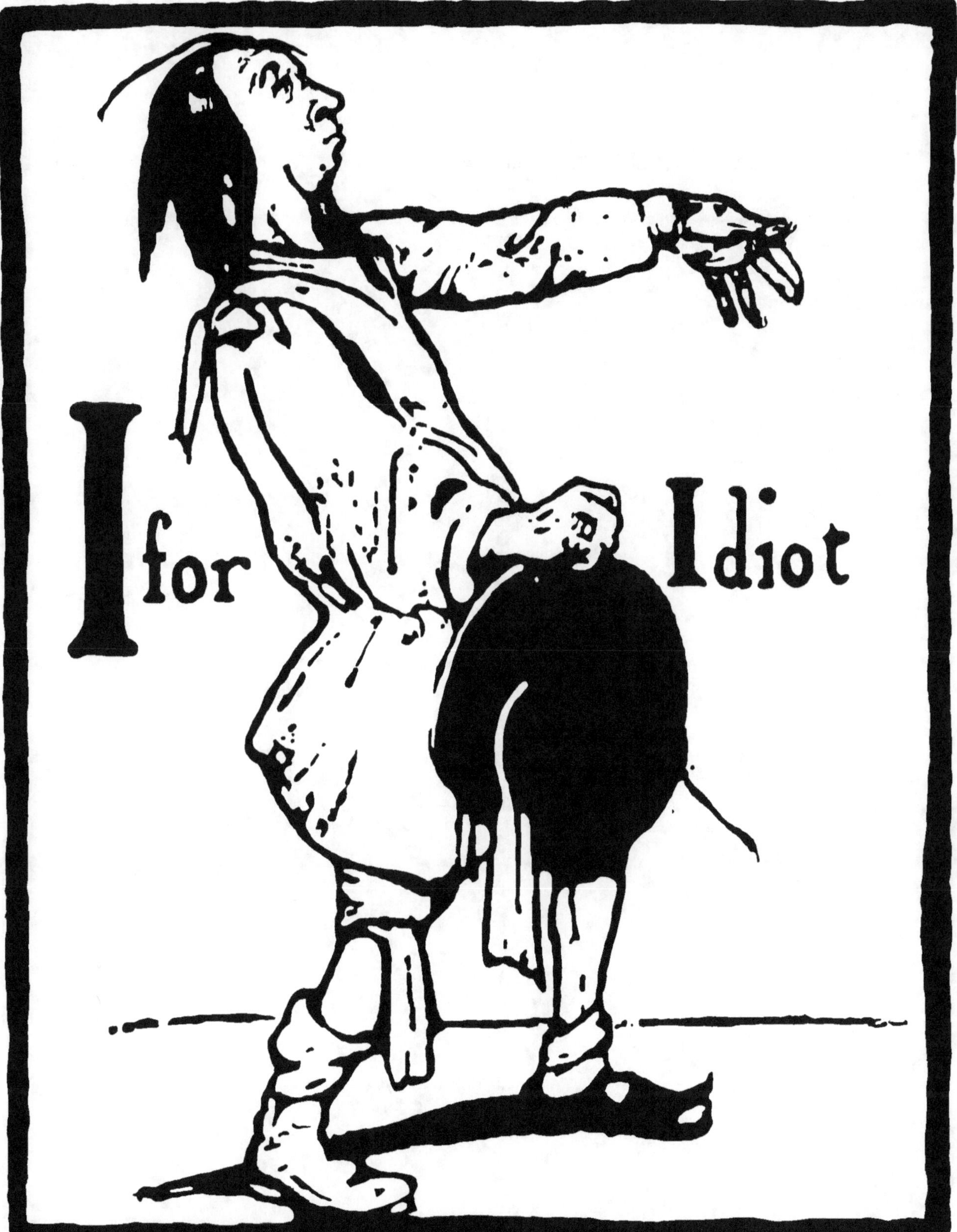

I for Idiot

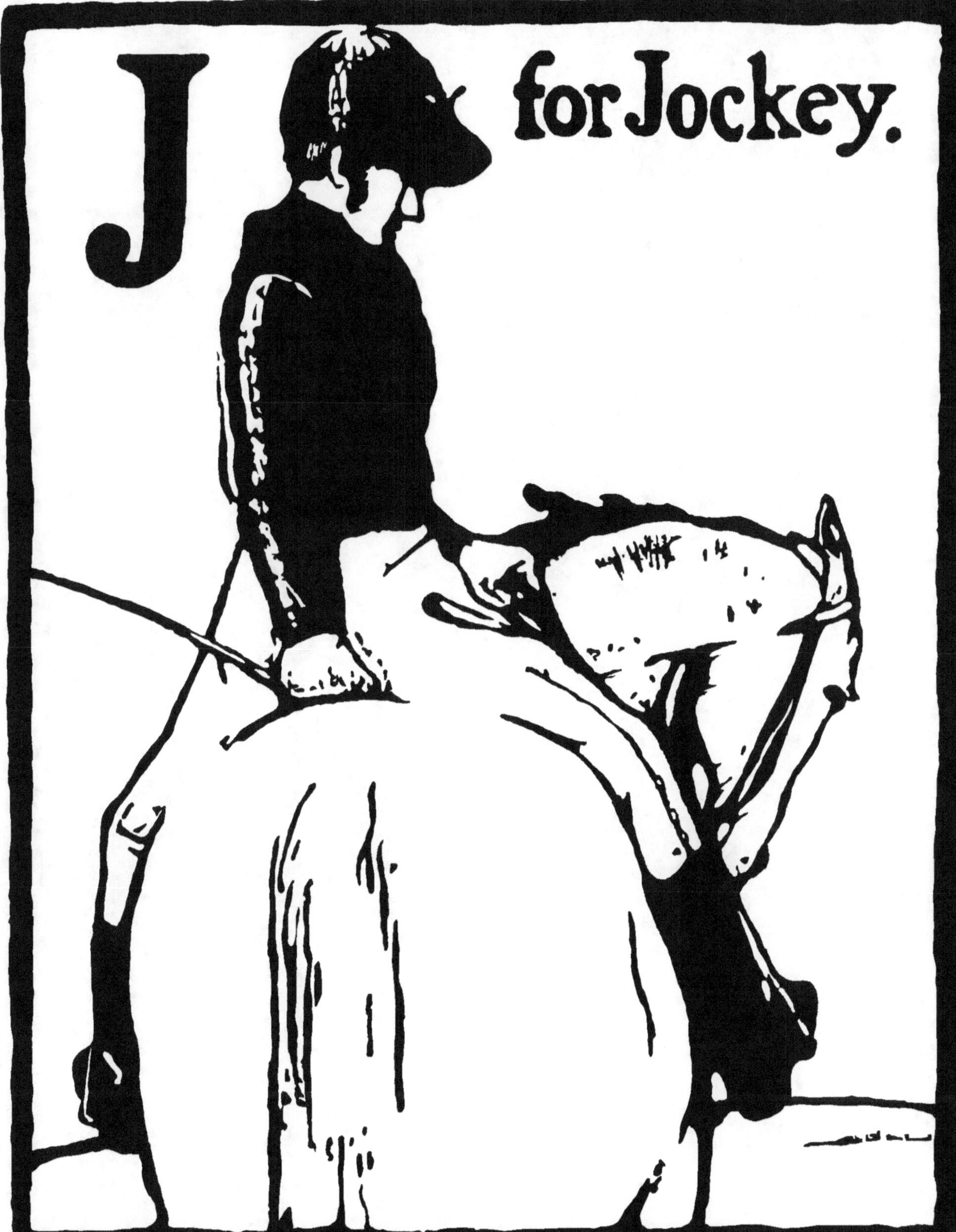

J
for Jockey.

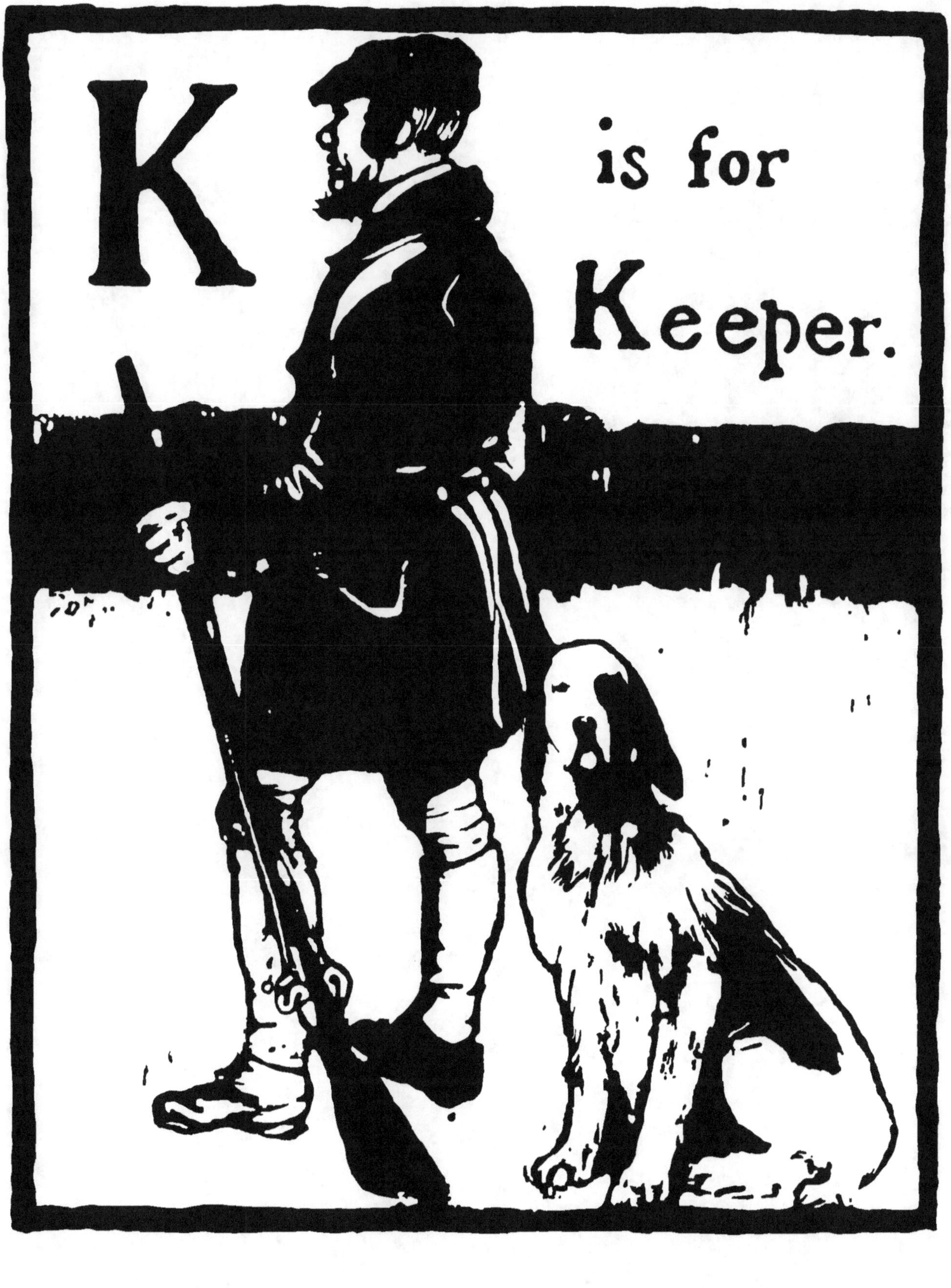

K
is for
Keeper.

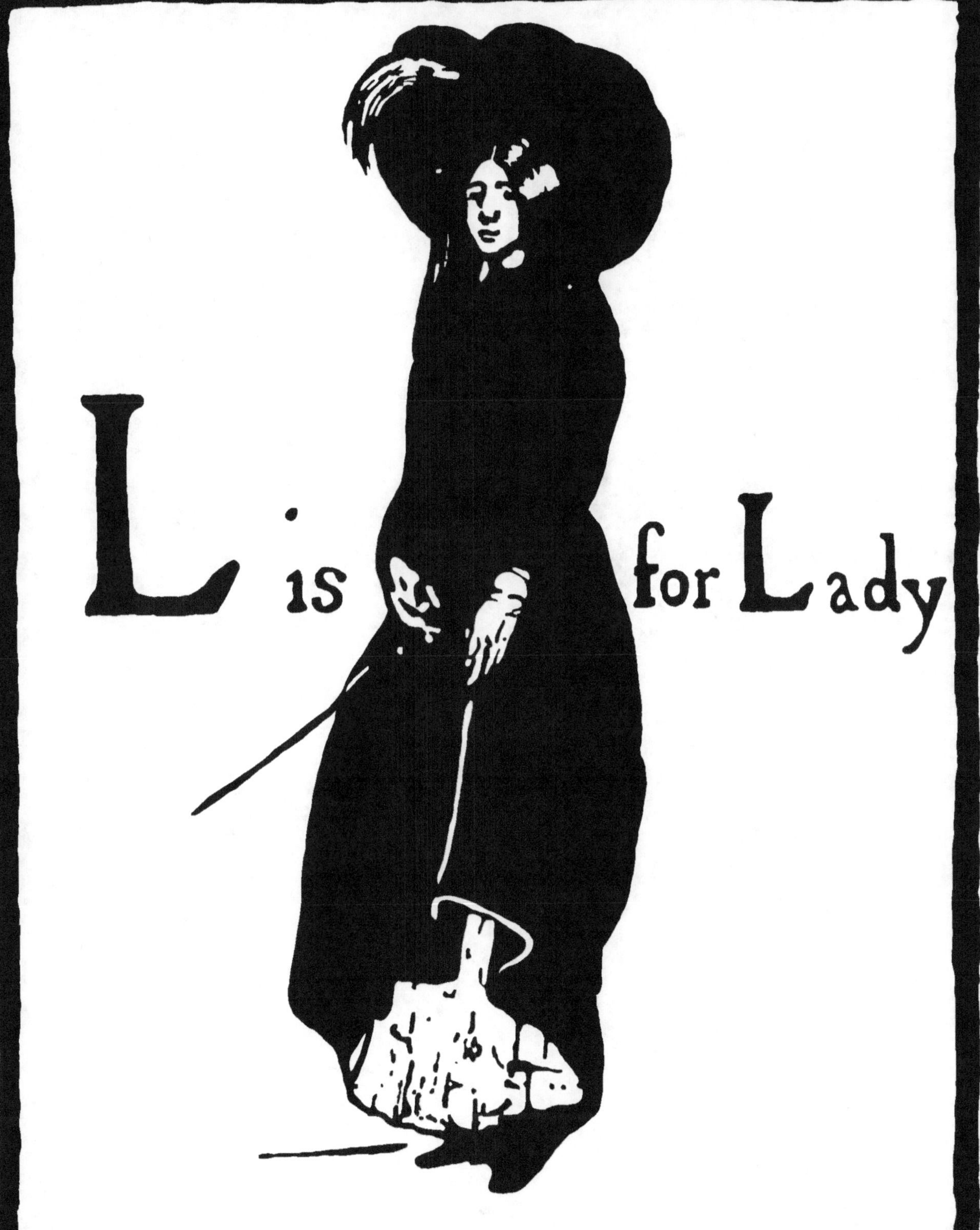
L is for Lady

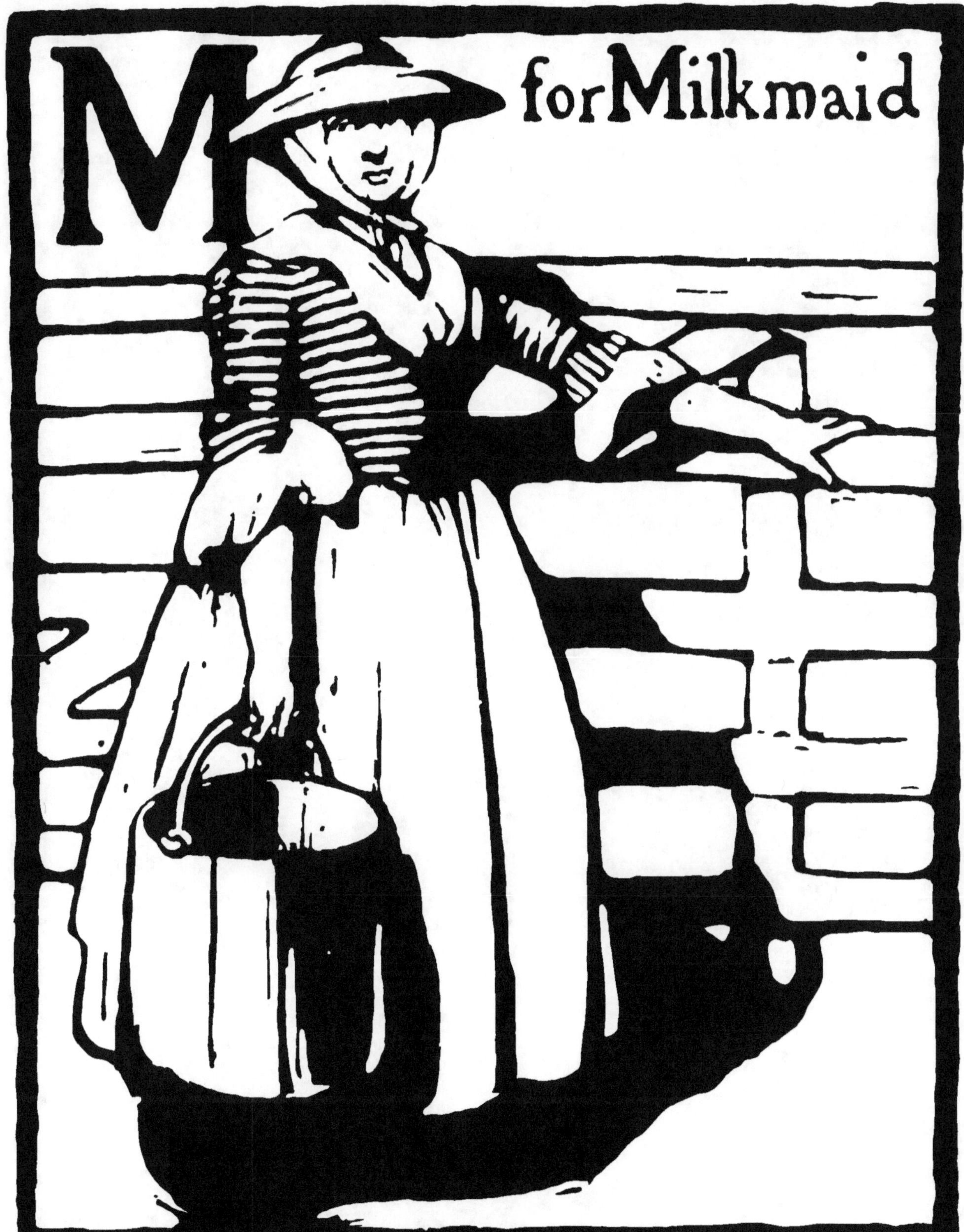
M
for Milkmaid

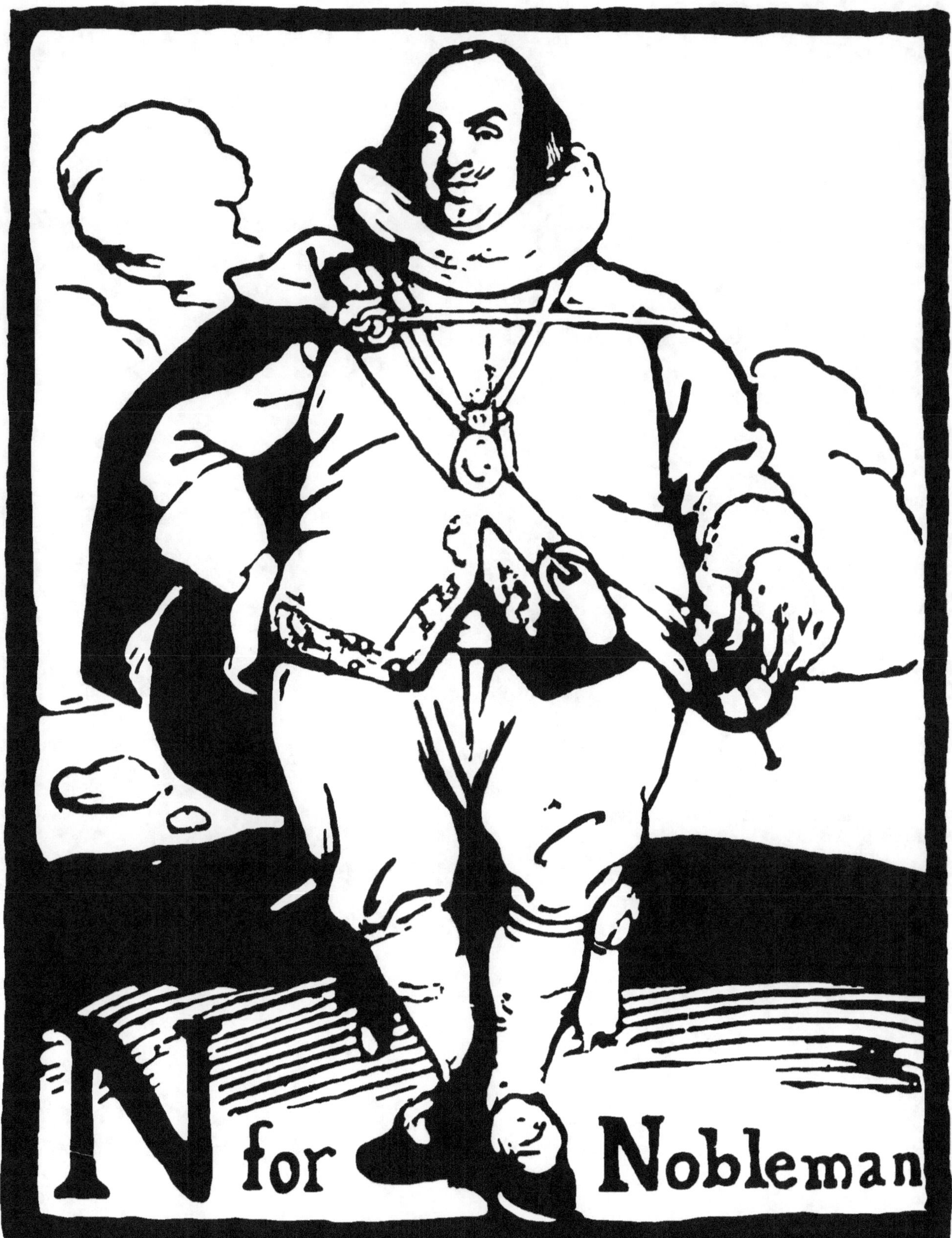

N for Nobleman

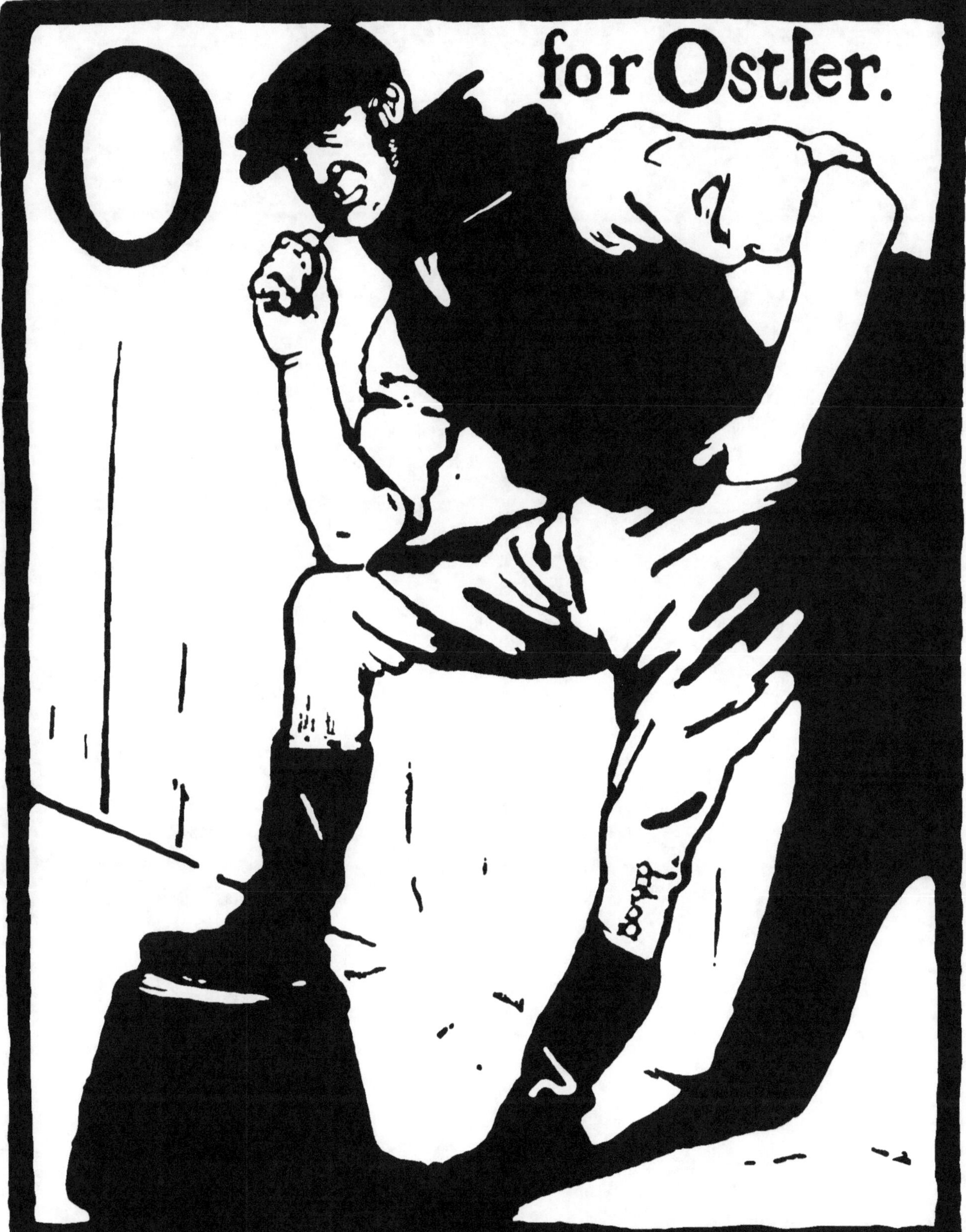
O
for Ostler.

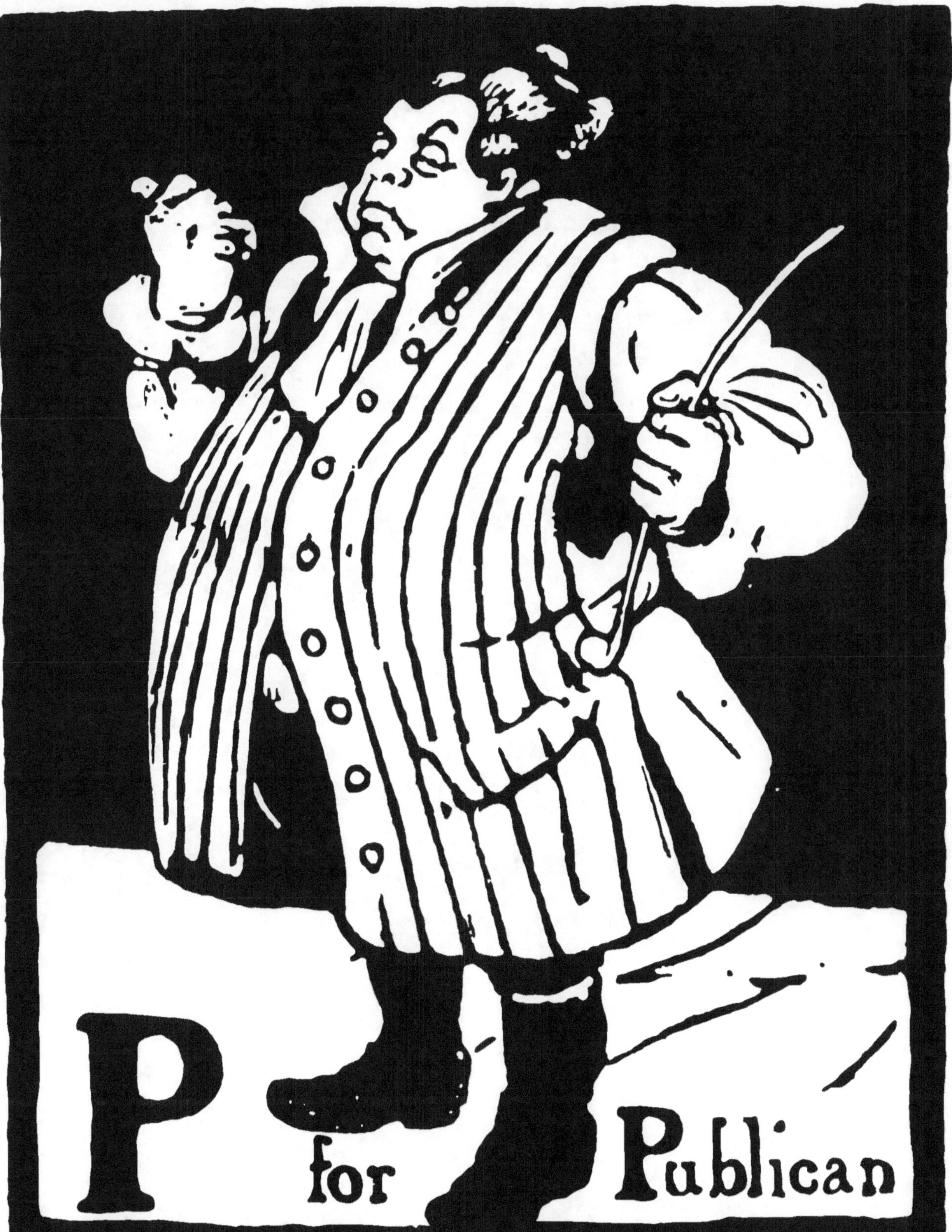

P for Publican

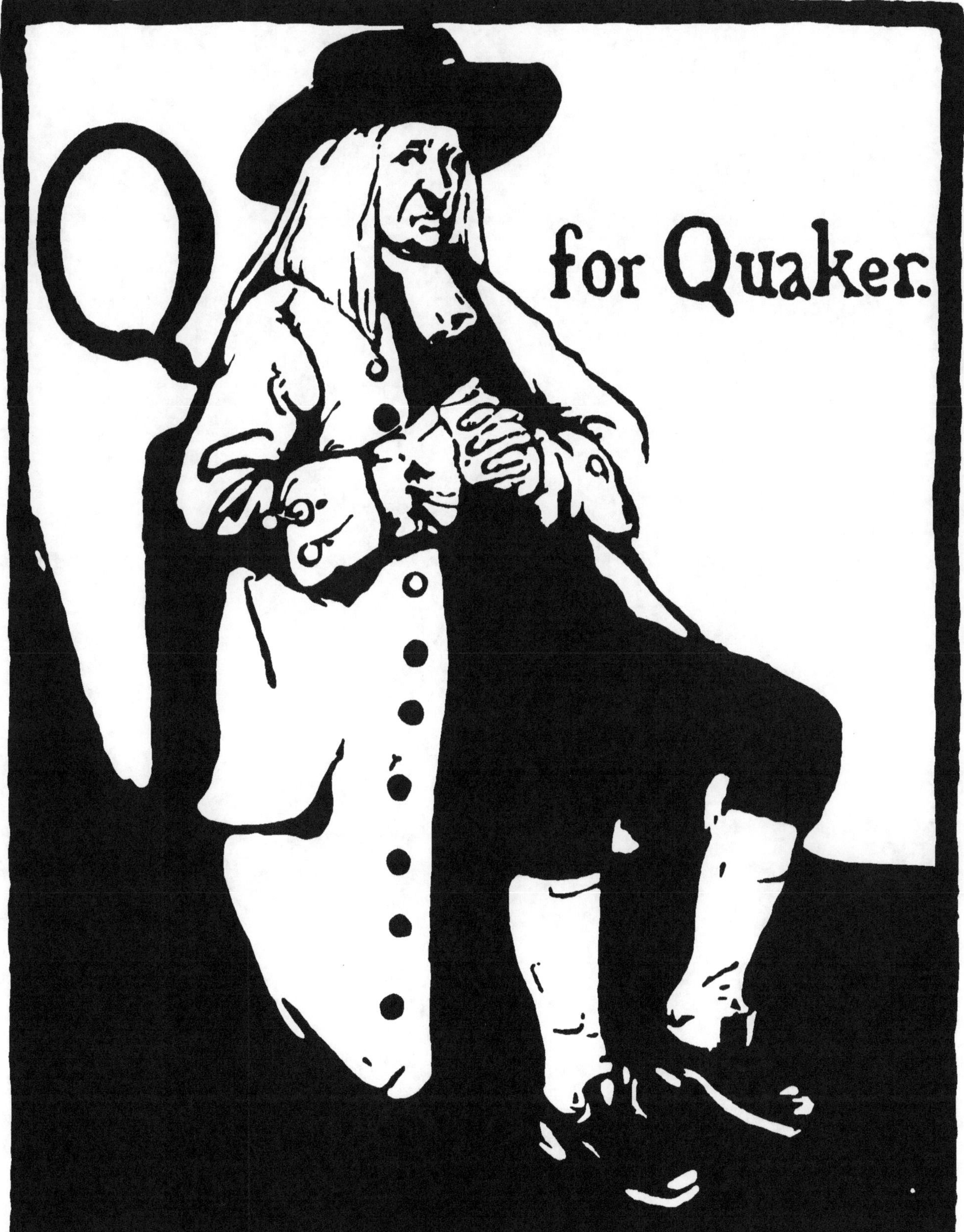

Q
for Quaker.

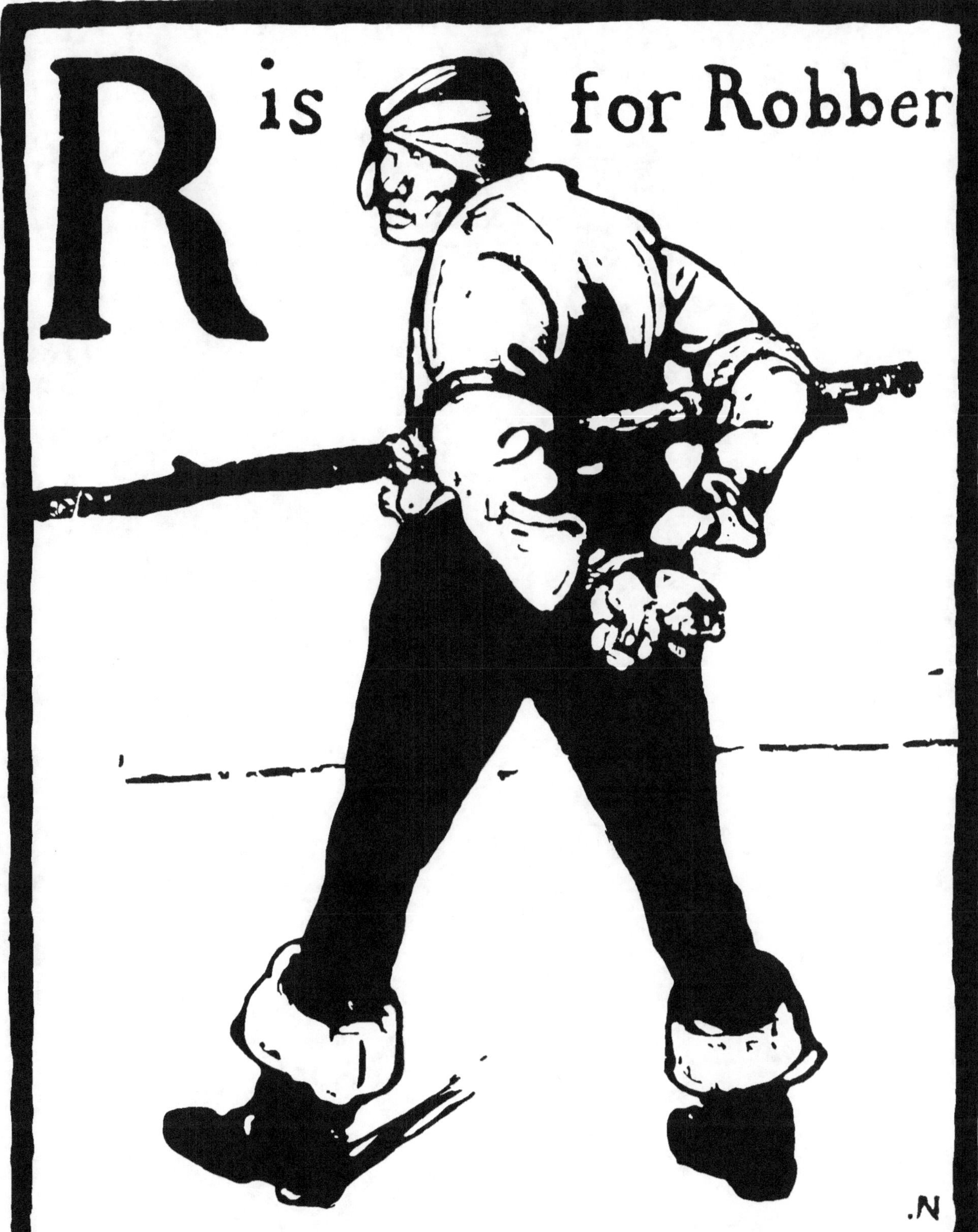

R is for Robber

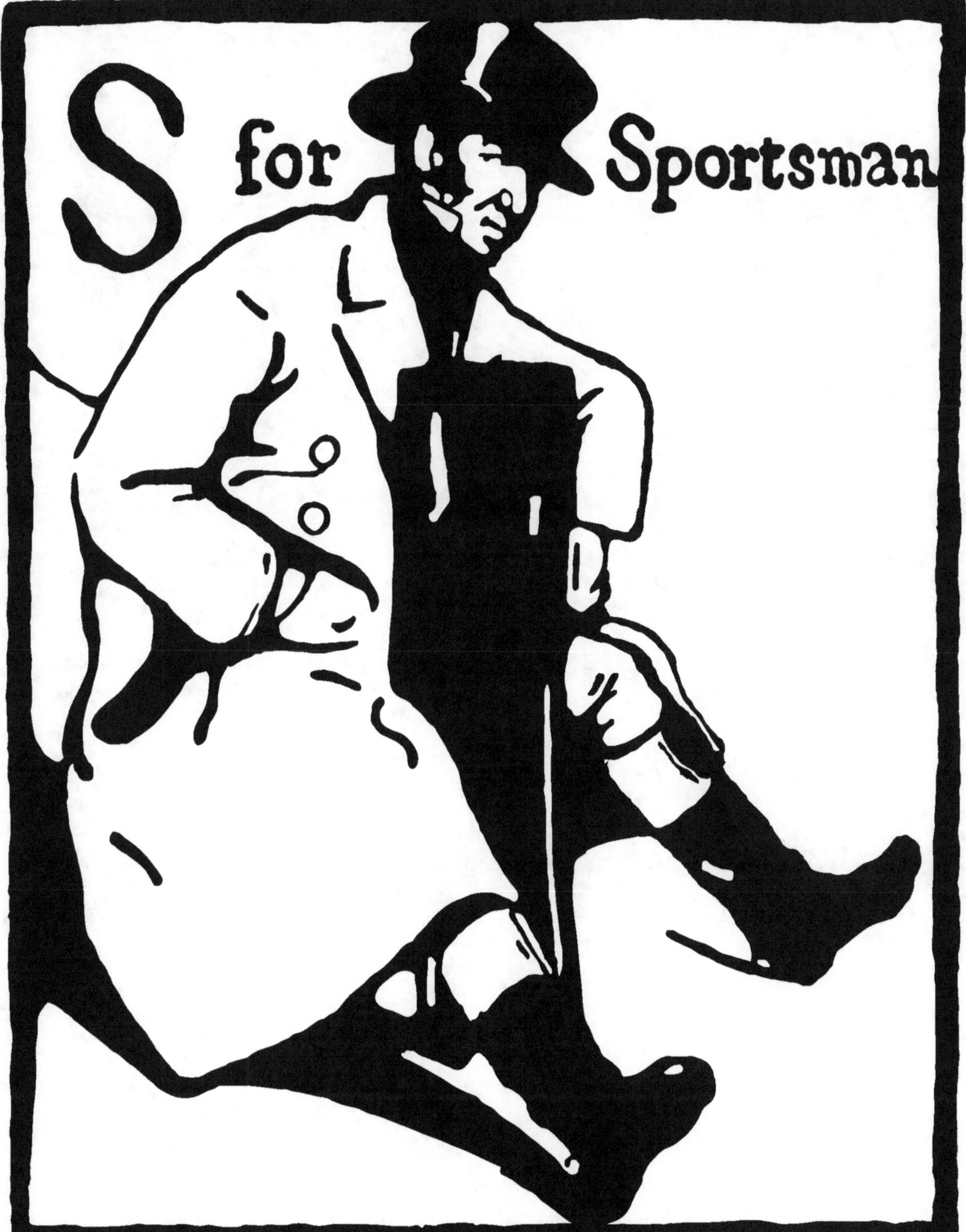
S for Sportsman

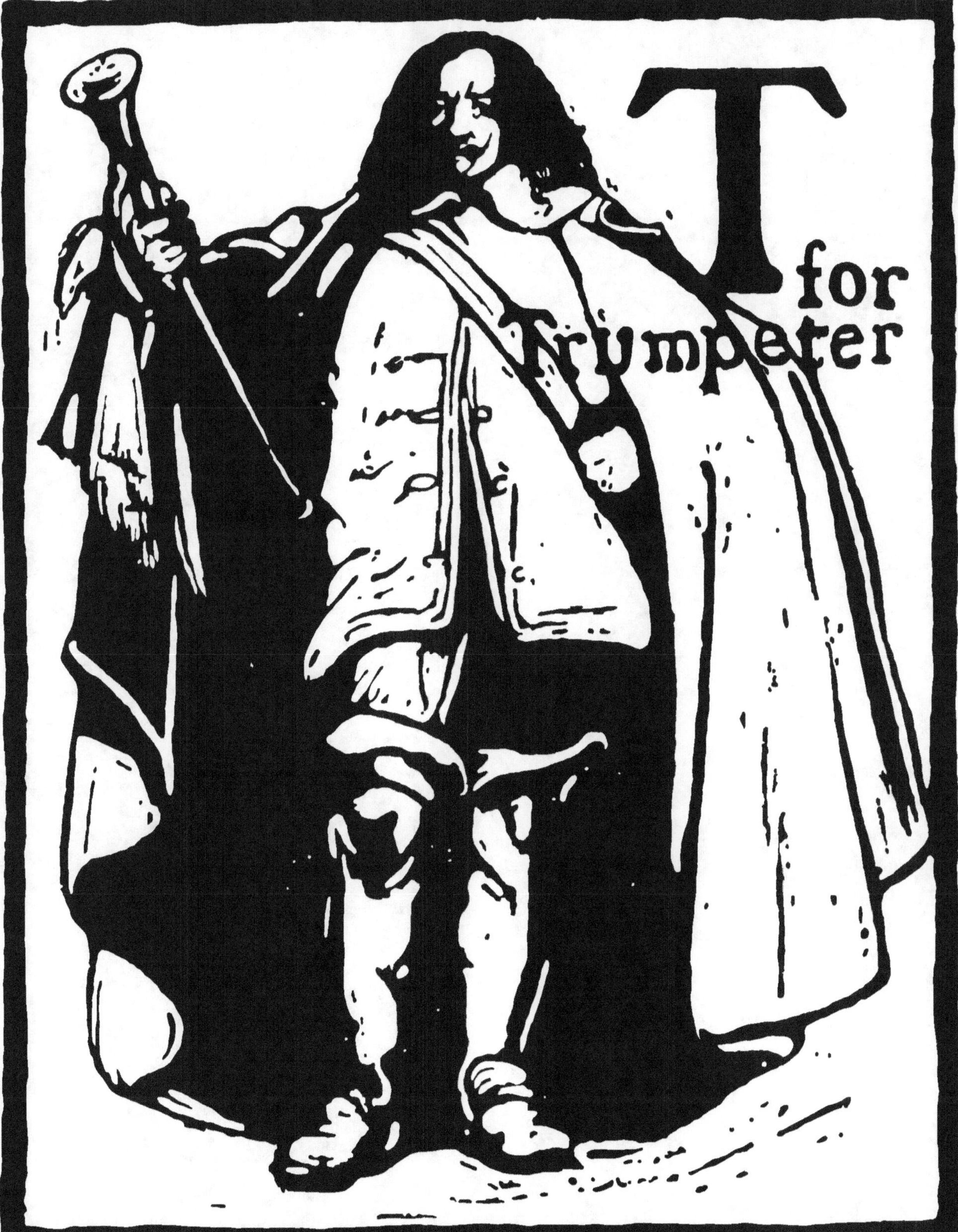

T
for
Trumpeter

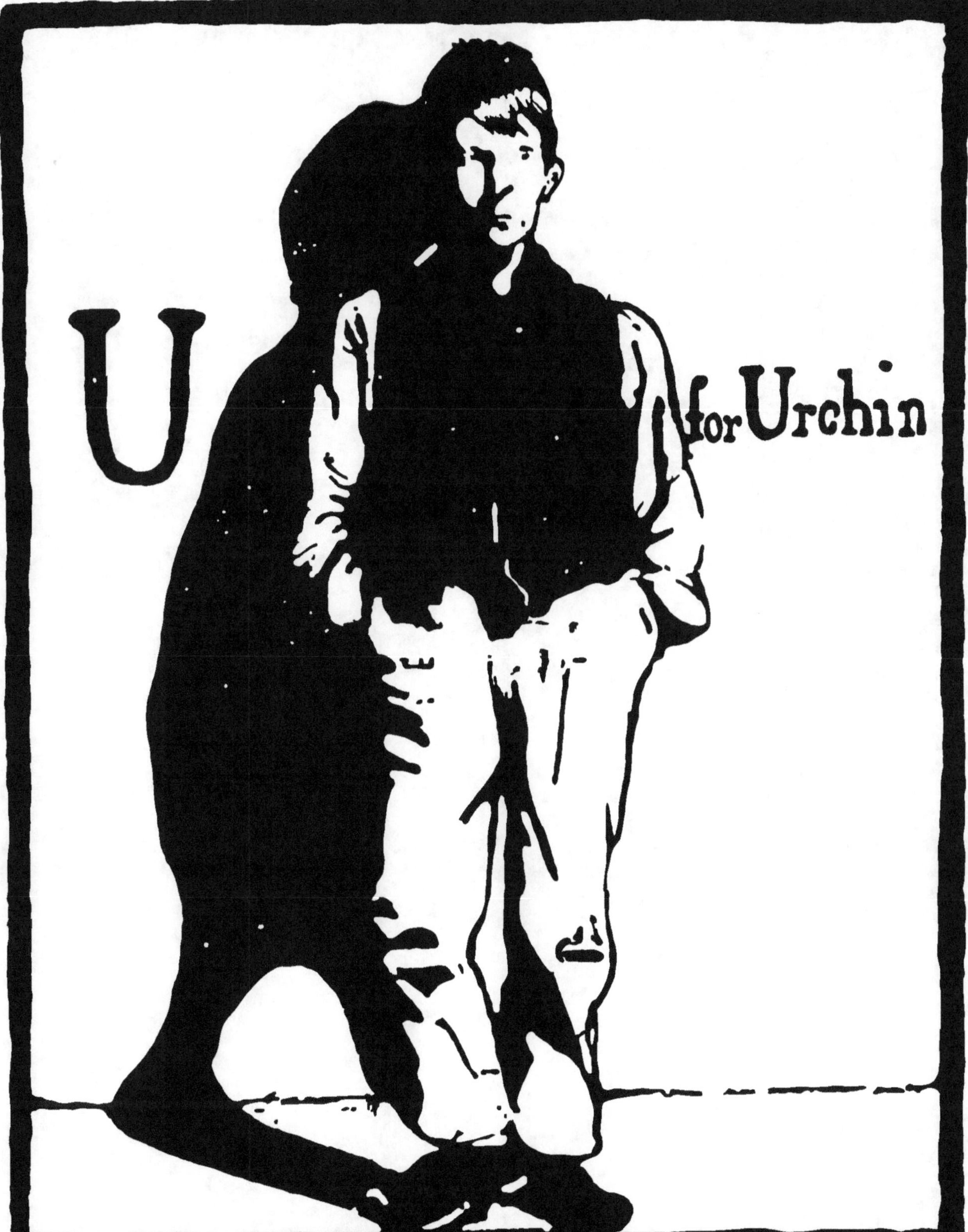

U
for Urchin

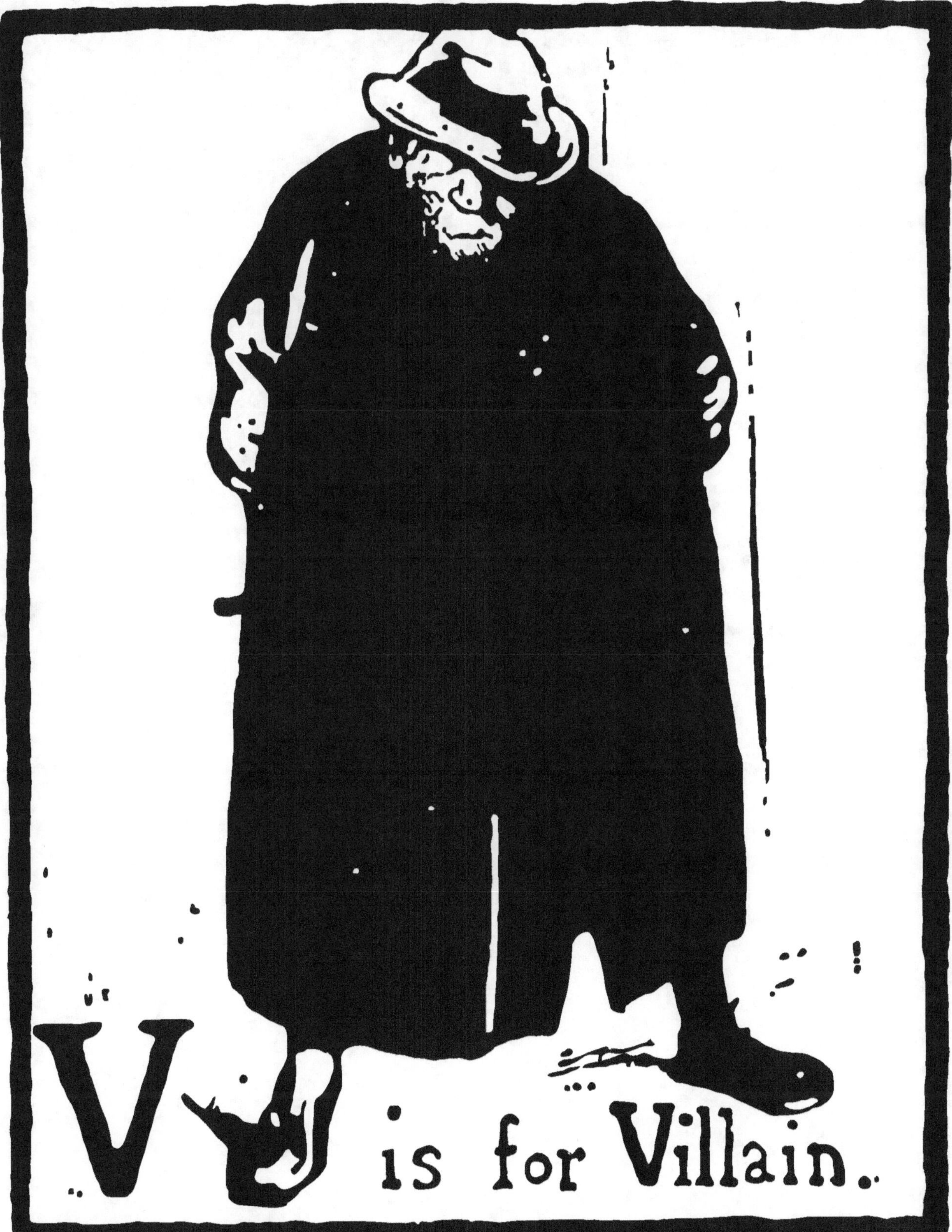
V   is for Villain..

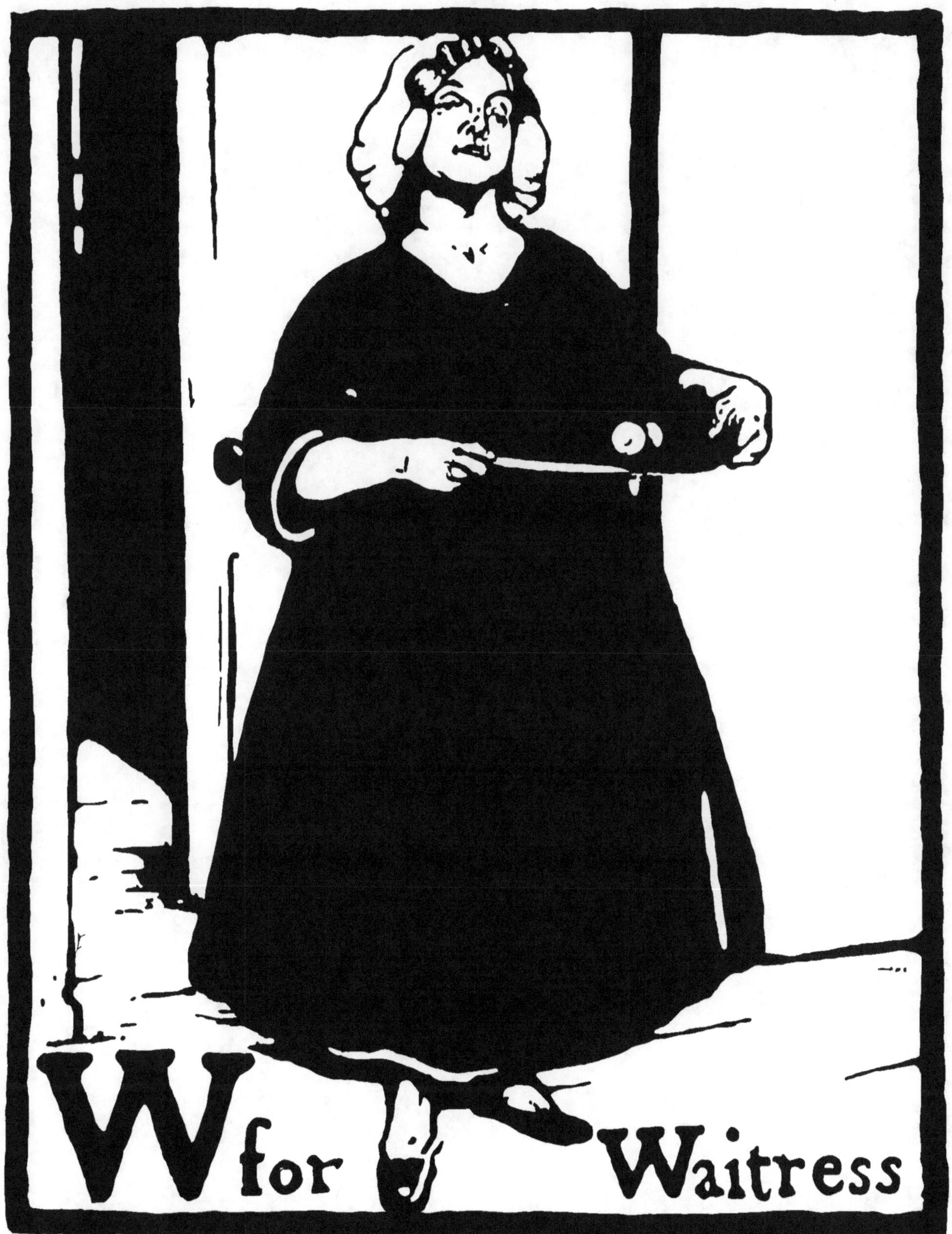

W for
Waitress

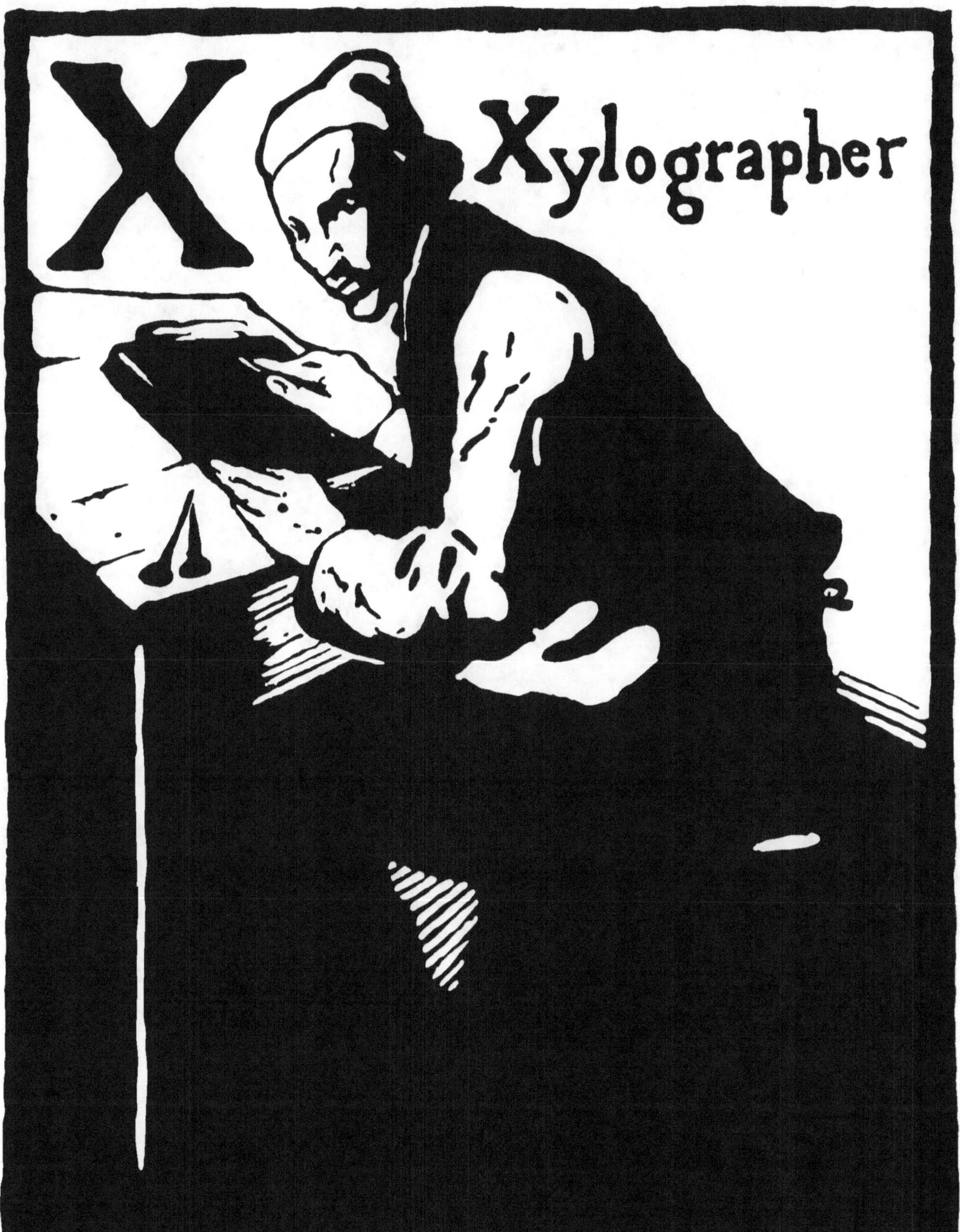

X
Xylographer

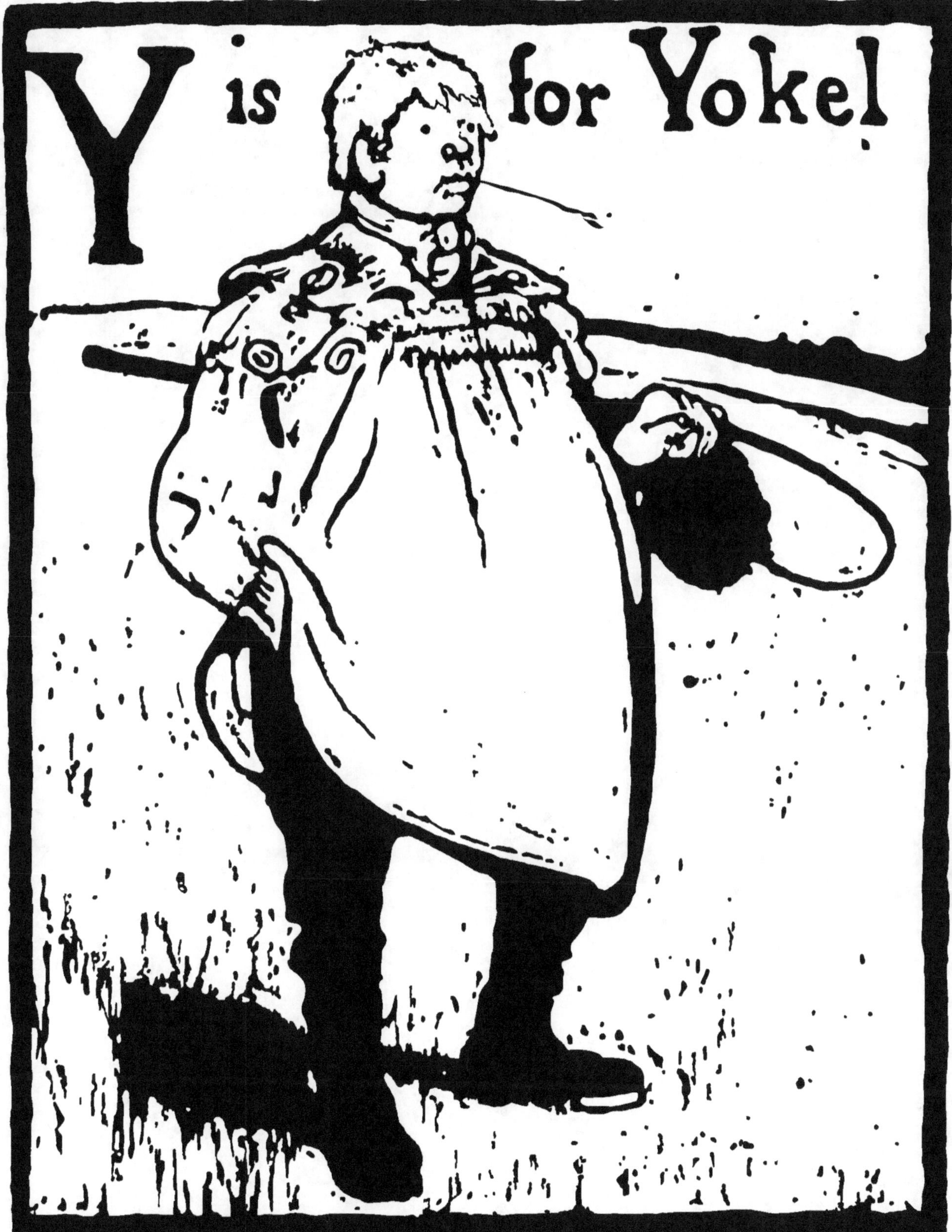
Y is for Yokel

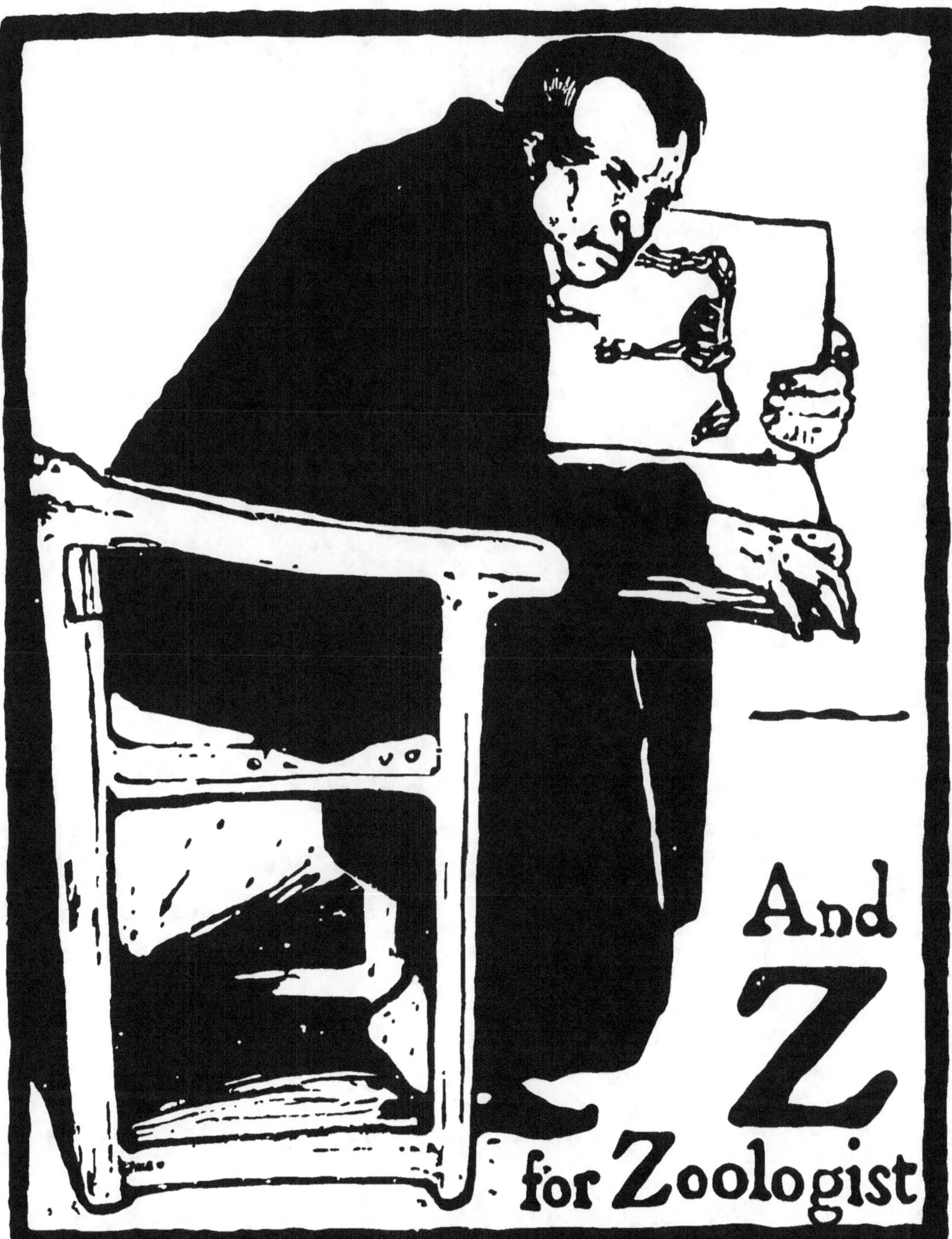

And
Z
for Zoologist

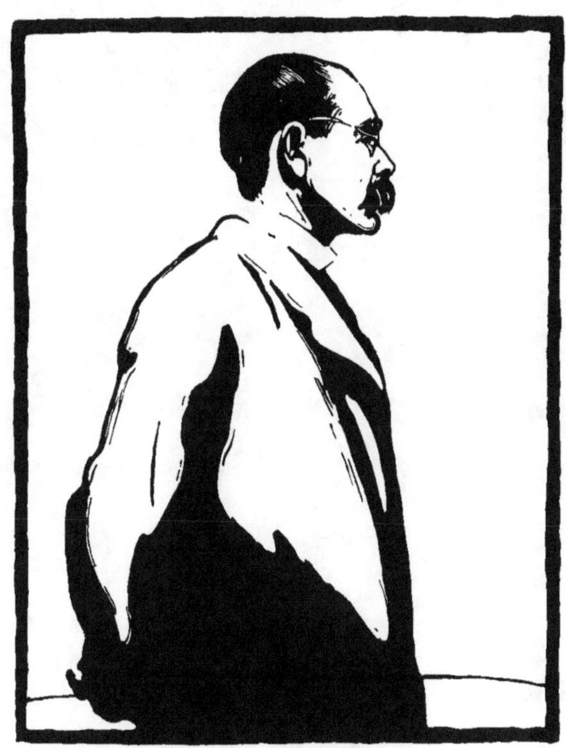

Rudyard Kipling.

If you have enjoyed this book, please look out for the following title:

Calendar & Character by William Nicholson

from Velluminous Press.